Activity Book for Children
Christopher Clark
Illustrated by Alex Brychta

4

banana

hit

net

peg

bat

glasses

clown

ice cream

shirt

tie

dirty

read

fox

jeans

hamburger

lift

rat

newspaper

feet

cap

dress

hat

jacket

shirt

skirt

sweater

sock

bag

umbrella

He can see a _____

She can _____

_____

I can see _____

_____

fat   cat   hat

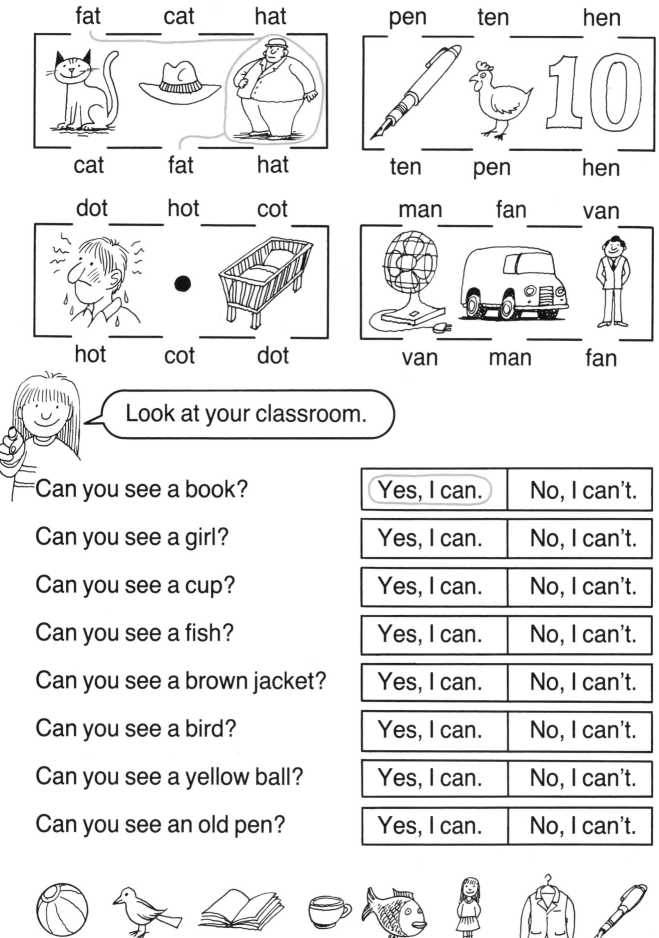

cat   fat   hat

pen   ten   hen

ten   pen   hen

dot   hot   cot

hot   cot   dot

man   fan   van

van   man   fan

Look at your classroom.

Can you see a book?	Yes, I can.	No, I can't.
Can you see a girl?	Yes, I can.	No, I can't.
Can you see a cup?	Yes, I can.	No, I can't.
Can you see a fish?	Yes, I can.	No, I can't.
Can you see a brown jacket?	Yes, I can.	No, I can't.
Can you see a bird?	Yes, I can.	No, I can't.
Can you see a yellow ball?	Yes, I can.	No, I can't.
Can you see an old pen?	Yes, I can.	No, I can't.

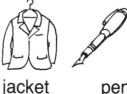

ball   bird   book   cup   fish   girl   jacket   pen

Bob is standing next to the door.
Liz is standing in front of the window.
Tina is standing between a boy and a girl.
Ron is standing behind a boy.
Jill is standing next to Ron.

He is standing in front of a boy.

She is standing_ _ _ _ _ _ _ _ _ _ _ _ a girl.

He is standing _ _ _ _ _ _ _ _ _ _ _ _ a boy.

She is standing_ _ _ _ _ _ _ _ _ _ _ _ a boy and a girl.

She is standing_ _ _ _ _ _ _ _ _ _ _ _ a girl.

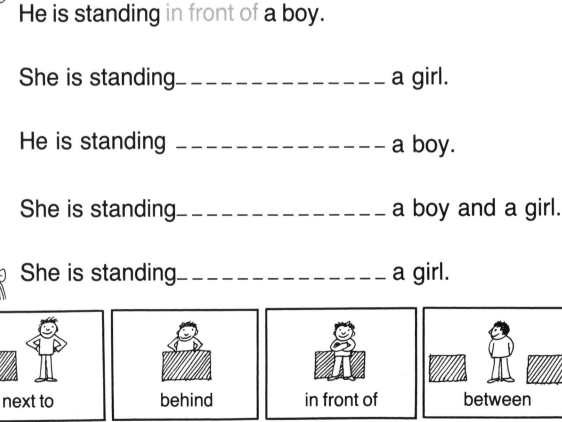

| next to | behind | in front of | between |

Draw Sam, Ben and Val.

Ben

Sam

Val

Val is standing _____

Sam _____

_____

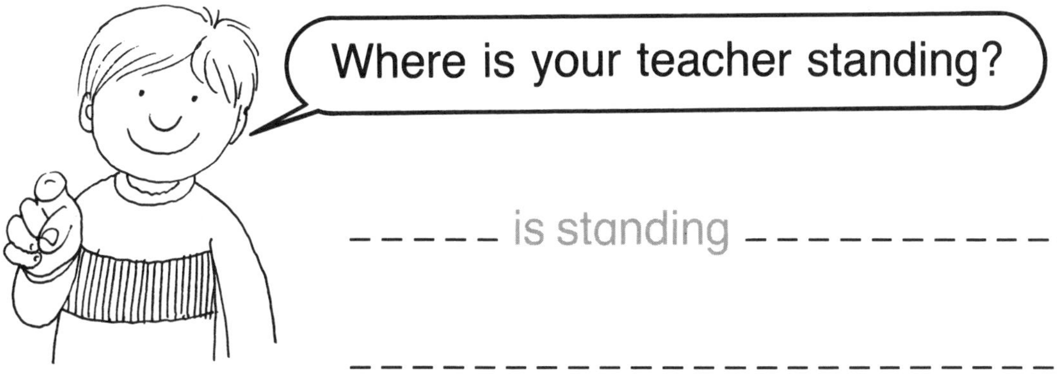

Where is your teacher standing?

_____ is standing _____

_____

P Pp

R Rr

F Ff

H Hh

Draw today's weather. ⇨

sunny windy raining snowing cloudy

My jeans are blue. My socks are white.
My shoes are blue and yellow.
My shirt is red and yellow.

Draw your clothes.

My _ _ _ _ _ _ _ _ _ _ _ _ _ _ _ _ _

_ _ _ _ _ _ _ _ _ _ _ _ _ _ _ _ _ _

_ _ _ _ _ _ _ _ _ _ _ _ _ _ _ _ _ _

_ _ _ _ _ _ _ _ _ _ _ _ _ _ _ _ _ _

black   blue   brown   green   orange

pink   purple   red   white   yellow

up			cut
cup			up
cut			nut
nut			cup

egg			peg
peg			ten
pen			pen
ten			egg

cap			fat
cat			cap
fat			cat
fan			fan

on			hot
dog			dog
dot			dot
hot			on

in			in
hit			sit
sit			hit
six			six

van			hat
fan			van
fat			fat
hat			fan

L Ll

E Ee

B Bb

D Dd

11 **12** **13** **14** **15**

16 **17** **18** **19** **20**

cat 14   van ____   bag ____   cap ____   man ____

pan ____   bat ____   fan ____   hat ____   car ____

CROSSWORD PUZZLE

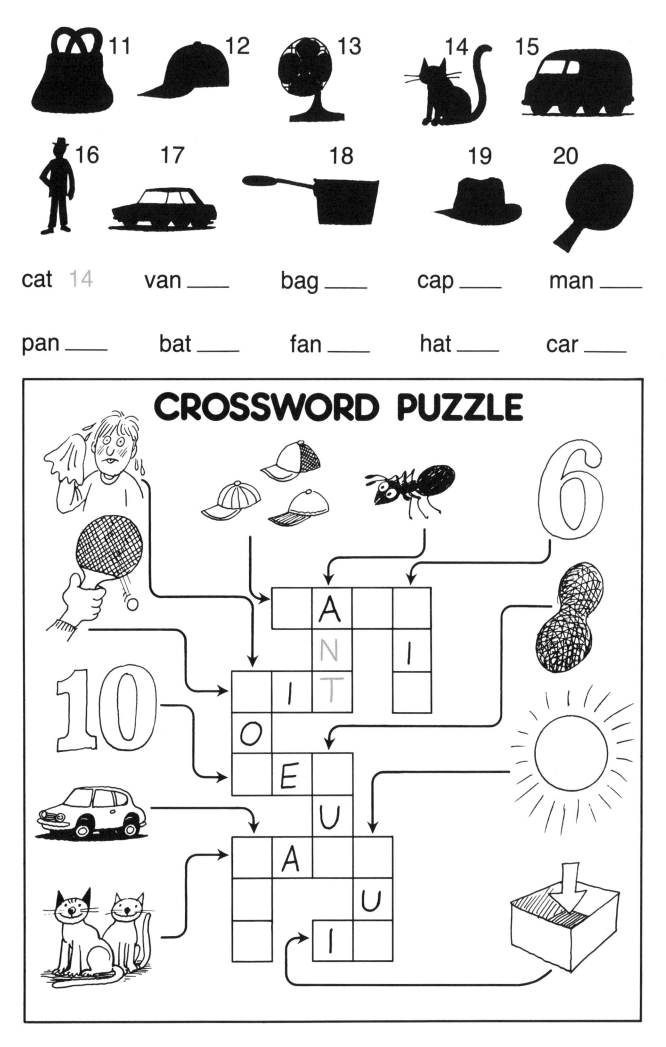

She can read. 　She can't read.

He can run fast.　They _ _ _ _ _ swim.

She _ _ _ _ _ spell.　He _ _ _ _ _ lift 100kg.

She _ _ _ _ _ spell.　They _ _ _ _ _ run fast.

What can you lift?

| _

What can't you lift?

_ _

Her hair is long.

His hair is short.

Her arms are long.

_ _ _ _ _ legs are short.

_ _ _ _ _ feet are little.

_ _ _ _ _ hands are big.

Her legs are short and fat.
Her feet are little.
Her arms are long and thin.
Her hands are big and fat.

Draw today's weather. ⇨

sunny   windy   raining   snowing   cloudy

⇦ Draw a clown.

His arms are _ _ _ _ _ _ _ _ _ _ _ _ _ _ _ _ _ _ _

_ _

_ _

_ _

_ _

Can you spell?

rat   _ a _   _ e _   _ i _   _ a _

_ o _   _ e _   _ a _   _ u _   _ i _

Aa	Bb	Cc	Dd	Ee	Ff	Gg	Hh	Ii	Jj	Kk	Ll	Mm
Nn	Oo	Pp	Qq	Rr	Ss	Tt	Uu	Vv	Ww	Xx	Yy	Zz

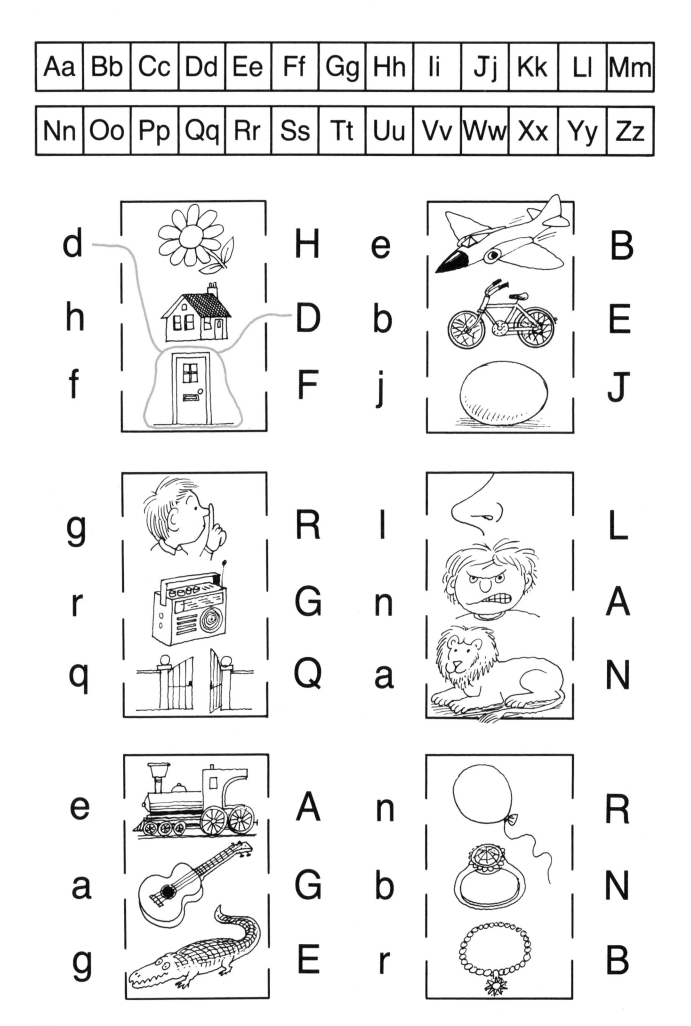

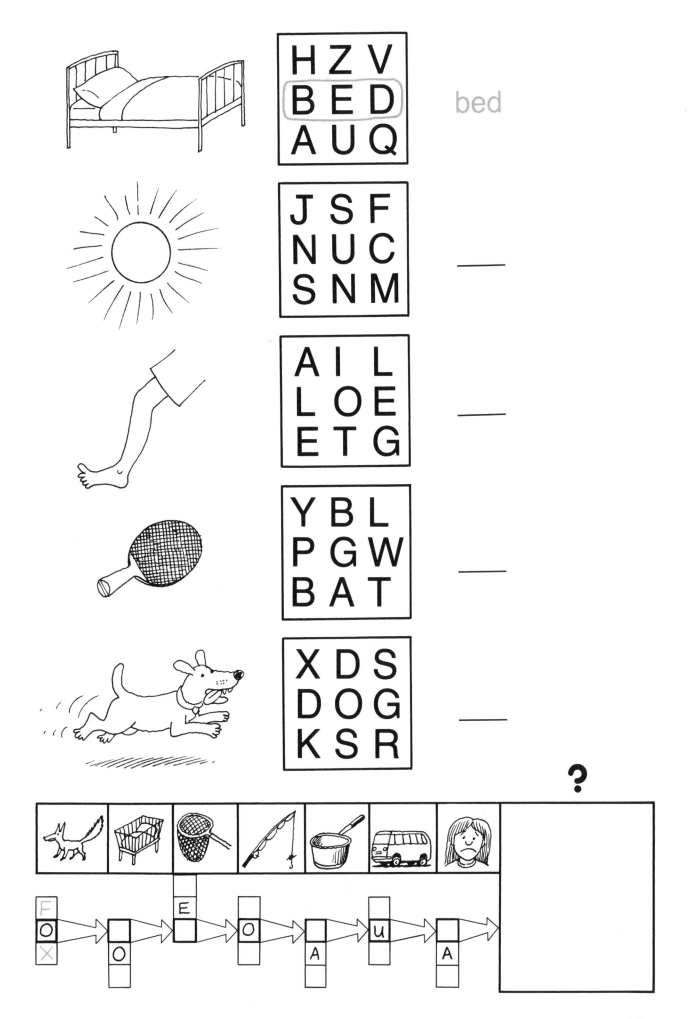

H	Z	V
B	**E**	**D**
A	U	Q

bed

J	S	F
N	U	C
S	N	M

___

A	I	L
L	O	E
E	T	G

___

Y	B	L
P	G	W
B	A	T

___

X	D	S
D	O	G
K	S	R

___

?

F		E			u	
O			O			
X	O			A		A

7.00

2.30

4.50

11.00

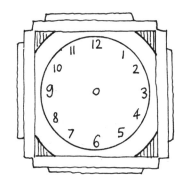

8.00

3.30

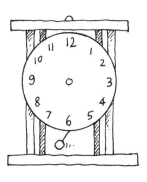

9.20

6.40

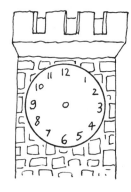

12.10

1.20

_ _ _ _

_ _ _ _

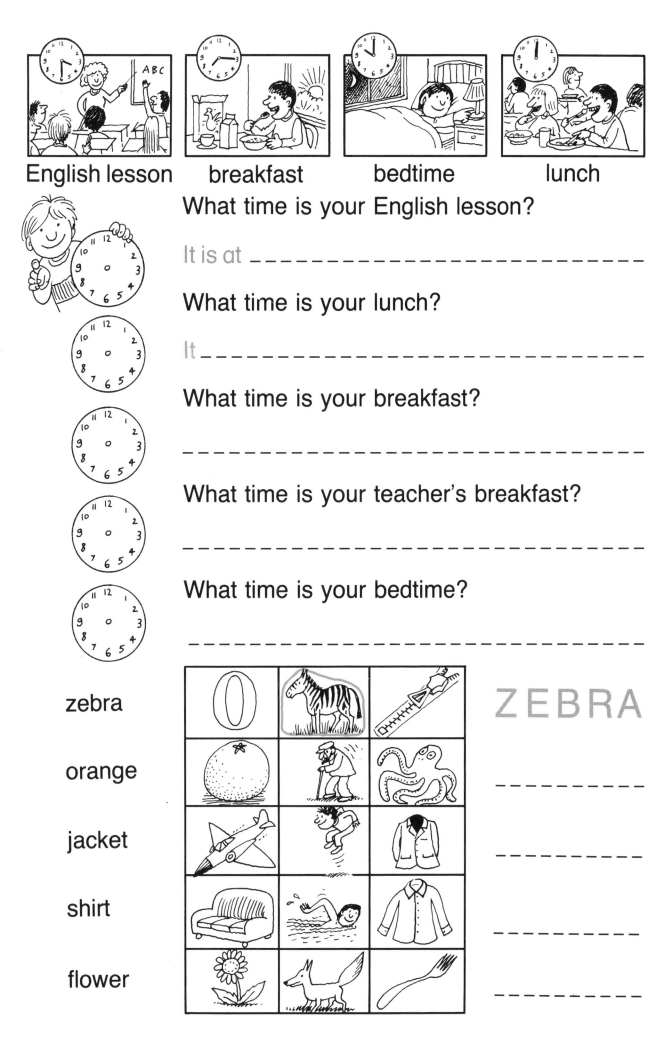

English lesson   breakfast   bedtime   lunch

What time is your English lesson?

It is at _

What time is your lunch?

It _

What time is your breakfast?

_ _

What time is your teacher's breakfast?

_ _

What time is your bedtime?

_ _

zebra

orange

jacket

shirt

flower

ZEBRA

_ _ _ _ _ _ _ _ _

_ _ _ _ _ _ _ _ _

_ _ _ _ _ _ _ _ _

_ _ _ _ _ _ _ _ _

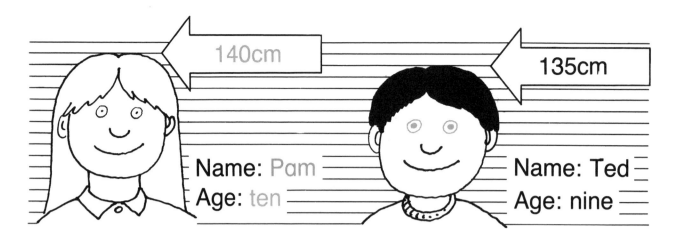

Name: Pam
Age: ten

Name: Ted
Age: nine

Her name is Pam.

She is ten.

Her hair is long and brown.

Her eyes are blue.

She is 140cm tall.

His name is _ _ _ _ _ _ _ _ _ _ _

He is _ _ _ _ _ _ _ _ _ _ _ _ _ _

His hair is _ _ _ _ _ _ _ _ _ _ _

His eyes are _ _ _ _ _ _ _ _ _ _

He is _ _ _ _ _ _ _ _ _ _ _ _ tall.

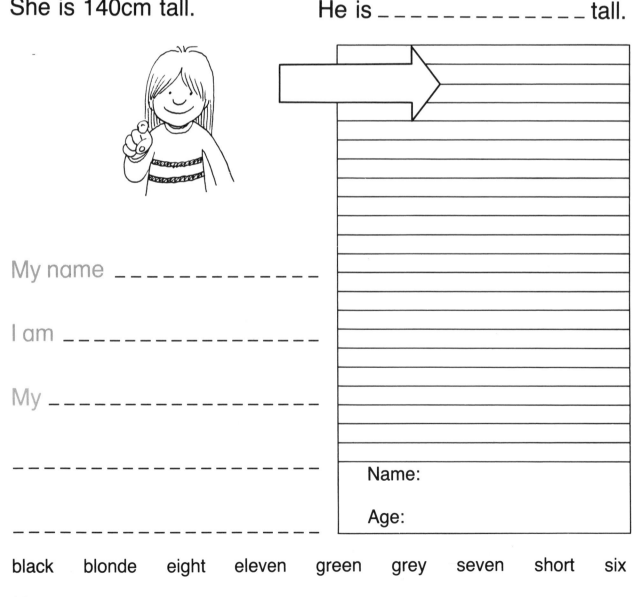

My name _ _ _ _ _ _ _ _ _ _ _ _ _

I am _ _ _ _ _ _ _ _ _ _ _ _ _ _ _

My _ _ _ _ _ _ _ _ _ _ _ _ _ _ _ _

_ _ _ _ _ _ _ _ _ _ _ _ _ _ _ _ _

_ _ _ _ _ _ _ _ _ _ _

Name:

Age:

black   blonde   eight   eleven   green   grey   seven   short   six

Draw today's
weather. ⇨

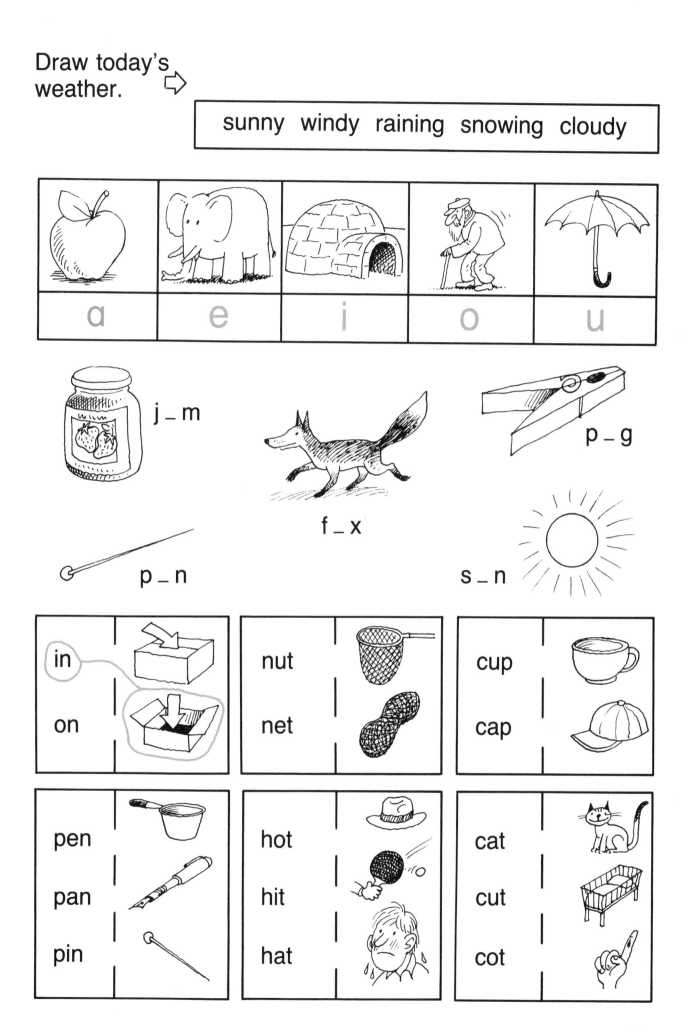

sunny windy raining snowing cloudy

a   e   i   o   u

j _ m

p _ g

f _ x

p _ n

s _ n

in
on

nut
net

cup
cap

pen
pan
pin

hot
hit
hat

cat
cut
cot

19

apples   bananas   hamburgers   ice creams   nuts   oranges   peaches

I can see three oranges

I can _____

_____

_____

_____

How many windows can you see?

I _____

one   two   three   four   five   six   seven   eight   nine   ten

eleven   twelve   thirteen   fourteen   fifteen   sixteen   seventeen   eighteen

I can eat five apples

I can eat _ _ _ _ _ _ _ _ _ _

She can eat _ _ _ _ _ _ _ _ _ _ !!

How many apples can you eat?   _ _ _ _ _ _ _

How many bananas can you eat?   _ _ _ _ _ _ _

How many hamburgers can you eat?   _ _ _ _ _ _ _

How many hamburgers can your teacher eat?   _ _ _ _ _ _ _

How many ice creams can you eat?   _ _ _ _ _ _ _

How many ice creams can your teacher eat?   _ _ _ _ _ _ _

match

radio   _ _ _ _ _ _ _ _ _ _

table   _ _ _ _ _ _ _ _ _ _

guitar   _ _ _ _ _ _ _ _ _ _

MATCH

21

His school is modern.
Their school is old and dirty.
Her school is big.
Our school is small.

Draw your school.

Our school _

Draw your classroom.

Draw your house.

My _

glasses heater newspaper picture reading shoes sleeping

fish eating cat bird banana baby

skirt television upside-down back to front

What is strange?

The man is wearing a _____

The dog _____

_____

_____

24

CAN YOU FIND THESE THINGS?

K	Y	H	D	O	G	F
F	R	O	Q	N	E	T
O	N	P	I	N	J	O
X	J	G	L	B	E	R
R	A	F	B	U	S	A
U	M	A	P	D	X	T

MEMORY GAME

Look at page 24. Then fold your book like this.

	Yes	No
Is the man wearing a tie?	Yes, he is.	No, he isn't.
Is the boy wearing a cap?	Yes, he is.	No, he isn't.
Is the girl wearing a ribbon?	Yes, she is.	No, she isn't.
Is the woman wearing a jacket?	Yes, she is.	No, she isn't.
Is the cat wearing a ribbon?	Yes, it is.	No, it isn't.
Is the boy wearing a jacket?	Yes, he is.	No, he isn't.
Is the woman wearing glasses?	Yes, she is.	No, she isn't.
Is the man wearing black shoes?	Yes, he is.	No, he isn't.

cap glasses jacket ribbon shoes tie

jump the highest   run the fastest

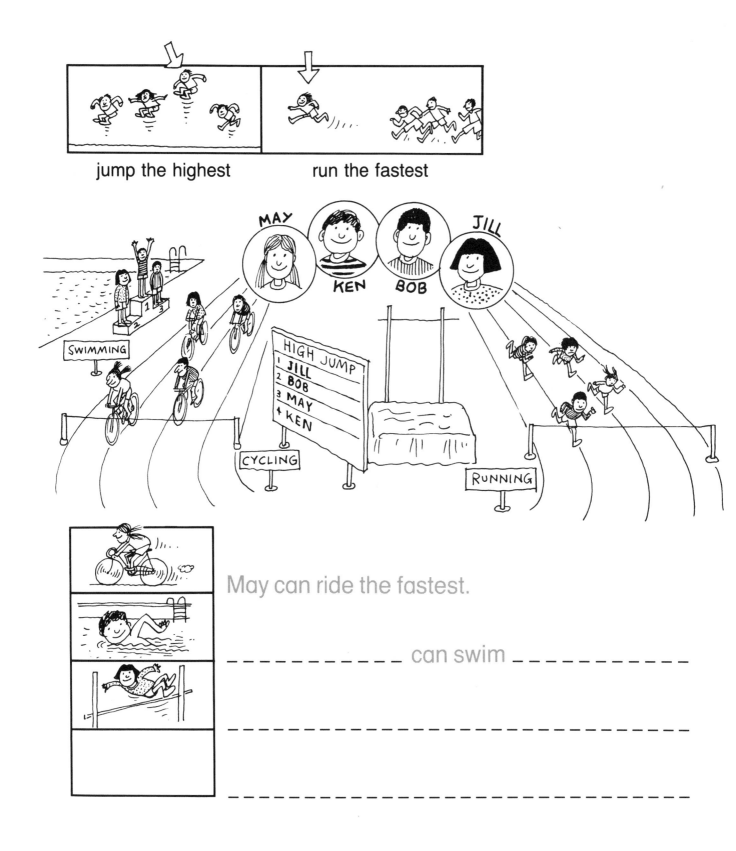

May can ride the fastest.

_ _ _ _ _ _ _ _ _ _ _ can swim _ _ _ _ _ _ _ _ _ _

_ _

_ _

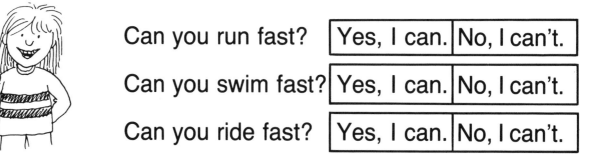

Can you run fast?	Yes, I can.	No, I can't.
Can you swim fast?	Yes, I can.	No, I can't.
Can you ride fast?	Yes, I can.	No, I can't.

mother   father   brother   sister   me

In your family:

Who can run the fastest?   My _ _ _ _ _ _ _ _ _ _ _ _ _ _ _

Who can read the fastest?   _ _ _ _ _ _ _ _ _ _ _ _ _ _ _

Who can jump the highest?   _ _ _ _ _ _ _ _ _ _ _ _ _ _ _

Who can sleep the longest?   _ _ _ _ _ _ _ _ _ _ _ _ _ _ _

Who can eat the fastest?   _ _ _ _ _ _ _ _ _ _ _ _ _ _ _

Draw this. ⇨

What is the opposite?

down	up	little	_ _ _ _ _	happy	_ _ _ _ _
cold	_ _ _ _ _	girl	_ _ _ _ _	thin	_ _ _ _ _

Draw a peg in front of the pan.
Draw a cat between the box and the pan.
Draw a cup on the box.
Draw a fan next to the jam.
Draw a pen in front of the jam.

What is on the box?   cup

What is in front of the jam?   _ _ _ _ _ _ _ _ _ _ _ _

What is behind the peg?   _ _ _ _ _ _ _ _ _ _ _ _

What is next to the box?   _ _ _ _ _ _ _ _ _ _ _ _

What is between the cat and the jam?   _ _ _ _ _ _ _ _ _ _ _ _

| behind | between | in front of | next to | on |

bird   BIRD

queen   _ _ _ _ _

panda   _ _ _ _ _

angry   _ _ _ _ _

28

Across ➡

1 Look at page 18.
What is the girl's name?

5 Look at page 21.
How many apples can the girl eat?

6 Look at page 28.
Is the cup on the box?

7 Look at page 9.
What is 18?

8 Look at page 28.
What is in front of the pan?

9 Look at page 24.
What is the man wearing?

10 Look at page 19.
How many umbrellas can you see?

Down ⬇

2 Look at page 23.
The boy's school is . . . .

3 Look at page 24.
What is the baby reading?

4 Look at page 22.
What colour are the girls' bikes?

9 Look at page 24.
What is the bird wearing?

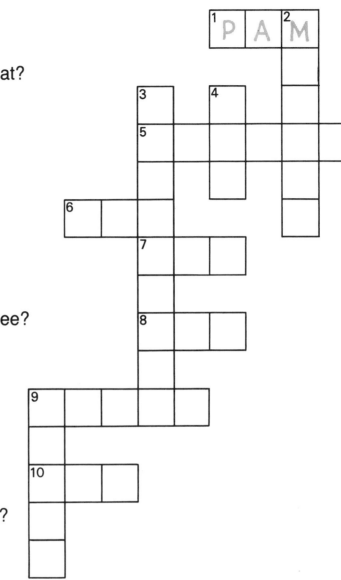

Can you find these things?

J A M A P A N T E N U T A L L E G

Draw today's ➯ weather.

| sunny windy raining snowing cloudy |

His   Her   My   Our   Their

Her hair is brown.

_ _ _ _ _ _ _ hair is black.

_ _ _ _ _ _ _ hair is red.

_ _ _ _ _ _ _ hair is brown.

_ _ _ _ _ _ _ hair is black.

rod	bed	sad
bus	jam	hen
net	cut	dot
pin	man	rat
map	fox	box
jet	hit	peg

He can swim.

He can't swim.

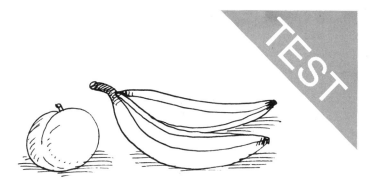

The peach is next to the bananas.
The peach is behind the bananas.

The girl is the tallest.
The boy is the thinnest.

It is 8:00.
It is 8:20.

She is wearing an old dress.
She is wearing a long skirt.

She can eat six apples.
She is eating an apple.

fish [F I S H]

bird [ ][ ][ ][ ]

hand [ ][ ][ ][ ]

gate [ ][ ][ ][ ]

queen [ ][ ][ ][ ][ ]

radio [ ][ ][ ][ ][ ]

31

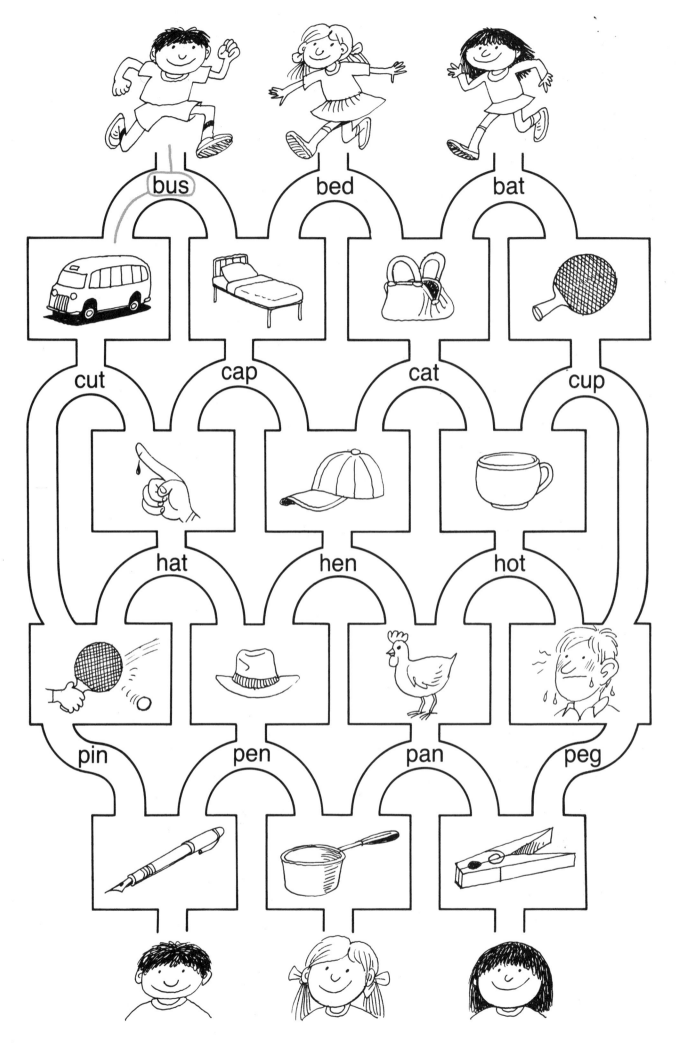

bus   bed   bat

cut   cap   cat   cup

hat   hen   hot

pin   pen   pan   peg